balancing life

my weekly planner

Michelle Dunn, PhD

with Emily Fanelli

tired dog publishing • new york

Tired Dog Publishing

10 Edgewood Avenue

Mount Vernon, New York 10552

First Printing 2017

Interior design by Emily Fanelli

Interior Illustrations by Emily Fanelli

ISBN 978-1-387-04032-2

Ordering Information:

Special discounts are available on quantity purchases by corporations, associations, educators, and others. For details, contact the publisher at the above listed address.

U.S. trade bookstores and wholesalers:

Please contact Tired Dog Publishing, Tel: (914) 663-6329

or email MDNeuropsych@gmail.com.

*To everyone who struggles to organize and
balance the many complex activites of life.
We understand.*

year

_____

name

_____

address

_____

_____

phone

_____

preface

We designed this planner for everyone who has felt overwhelmed in their efforts to lead a balanced life in which responsibilities are met, there is time to socialize, eat, sleep, exercise, and relax.

We know many bright, talented people who struggle with time management to the extent that it prohibits them from achieving their academic, occupational, or social potential. Poor organization and planning threaten life satisfaction. People struggle to meet their responsibilities and balance their time in many ways and for many reasons.

Anna makes "to-do" lists each day including all of the tasks she thinks must be accomplished on that day and in the near future. She prioritizes the tasks but usually ends up overwhelmed because she is looking at such a mountain of work. Her "to-do lists" include many of the same tasks day after day because it has been impossible for her to get to them. Some days she even writes multiple to do lists and obsesses about what she needs to do. Some days the mountain of work makes her anxious enough that she freezes and accomplishes little to nothing. This planner can break this cycle because it promotes the effective strategy of "one thing at a time" and promotes learning how much can realistically be done in one day.

Ben uses a planner every day. He writes down all of his homework, chores, and appointments. He writes due dates for long-term assignments. He even writes things such as "study for math midterm" or "work on history essay" but he does  not break down the task into separate, specific steps that could be completed on separate days. Sometimes he does not get enough done well in advance of the dues date. The due date creeps up on him and then he panics. He is not prepared for the big test or he rushes through completing an essay. This planner promotes specifying what step in a long-term task will be completed on each given day so due dates don't creep up.

Jake writes down his assignments, even breaking up long-term assignments. He records his appointments and chores. Yet he has trouble getting everything done because he gets distracted by his favorite activities, which include going online to watch videos, play games, read, look at social media, and texting him friends. He does not plan his free time. This planner encourages people to actually plan free time and balance it with other activities.

Laurie works hard in school and plans to get a lot done each day but she tends to leave certain assignments until the last minute. She says that sometimes a friend will call her to get together and she cannot go because she has to complete work due the next day. Sometimes she just decides to go out, convincing herself she doesn't really need to study for that test tomorrow. Laurie does not plan for the unexpected, so sometimes she misses out on social events or does poorly in school. One Friday she had a report due, which had been assigned weeks ago. She waited until the day before to do it and then got a nasty virus. Her teacher told her that was no excuse, since she had 3 weeks to complete the report. This planner actually helps people anticipate the unexpected by seeing due dates and making a written plan to get the work done well in advance.

Some people have trouble balancing all of life. Isabelle has a demanding job where she often takes work home to complete it. She works all of the time and says she has no time for anything else. She is successful in doing all of the work and chores listed in her calendar on her phone but she has no time left to relax or socialize. Debra uses two separate planners. One is for work and for chores and the other is for socializing and appointments. She often does not have enough time to complete all of the work she plans to do at home because she does not plan it with her appointments in mind. She does not coordinate her plans for all of her activities. So she goes to her appointments and does not get to the other work. This planner helps to coordinate and balance time spent on ALL aspects of life.

This planner is made for all of us. It can help with problems of trying to fit too much into one day or procrastination due to feeling overwhelmed. It can help the user: 1) employ the adaptive strategy of doing one thing at a time, 2) learn the amount that can realistically be accomplished in one day, and 3) plan for the unexpected.

We hope it brings balance to your busy life.

sincerely,

michelle & emily

introduction

_____

how to use this planner

You will notice that this planner is a little different from typical planners. There are no time slots. Every day of the week has just as much room as any other (in other planners, Saturday and Sunday usually have less space… as if there is less to do on the weekends!). Here, each day is divided into 3 columns.

The purpose of this planner is to learn to realistically manage short-term and long-term projects, while balancing the time devoted to those projects with the time devoted to chores, appointments, free time, and social life.

why 3 columns?

Each day is divided into three columns for three types of activities.

In column one, you will write all short-term assignments, specifically activities that must be completed by the next day.

In column two, you will write due dates/deadlines for long-term assignments on the date they are due, and highlight them in yellow. On the dates leading up to these deadlines, you will write the steps in task analyses for these long-term assignments. Examples of long term assignments are papers/reports, tests where one has multiple days to study, a presentation, or a project requiring construction. For any long term project, the first step is to do the task analysis enumerating all steps for completing the project. See the list below for an example of the steps in a task analysis for writing a paper.

10 STEPS FOR WRITING A PAPER

1. Think of an idea based on the question

2. Do preliminary research about the topic

3. Develop and write the thesis (e.g., "This is so because of ____, ____, and ____.)

4. Make an outline (linear or graphic organizer, whatever works best)

5. Thoroughly research the topic and take notes (get facts, examples, quotations to provide support for points. Be sure to record references and link them to facts so it is clear where each fact came from).

6. Modify outline based on anything new learned

7. Write first draft

8. Proofread and edit

9. Final draft

10. Bibliography

There are a number of natural points to check in with the professor/teacher (e.g., after writing the thesis and outlining and after the first draft is complete). You will enter these appointments into column three.

Each step in the task analysis for writing a paper would be written on a specific day in column two. More than one step can be written on a single day or steps such as "Thoroughly research the topic and take notes" can be divided over multiple days if necessary. The idea is to schedule all of the steps so that the long-term project is completed ahead of the due date.

In column three you will enter appointments, chores, free time and social gatherings. When you write in your appointments, make sure to include the time, place, and person with whom you will meet. Definitely plan free time so that you can balance it with all the rest.

why no time slots or dates?

Unless an appointment or a class, it is rare that tasks in our lives must be carried out at a specified time. When we plan our time, it usually is the case that we decide on what must be completed by the end of each day. This includes activities to be completed during work time or school or after work/school.

You will see that there are no dates in this planner. You will write them into the box to the right of the day of the week.

why a week-at-a-glance?

Looking at a week in one glance allows one to balance activities over the entire week. For example, chores are scheduled at a time when there is less pressure to complete work assignments (in columns 1 and 2). Work on long-term assignments can be planned around a social gathering.

learning how to realistically estimate task time

When someone is first learning to plan their time, it is often the case that he or she overestimates the amount that can be done in a given timeframe. In other words, the amount of time a task takes is grossly underestimated. There are two recommended strategies for learning to correctly estimate time. The first is to write time estimates in parentheses next to each task and then write the actual amount of time the task took next to the initial estimate. The second method is to cross out any task not completed on a given day in red and move it to another day (before it is due) and highlight it in green. This color coding will instantly give you an idea of how successful you are in completing tasks on time. If there is a lot of red it means that you are overestimating what can realistically be completed in the time allotted OR it indicates procrastination.

a word about pressure and anxiety

Planning with balance in mind and following a plan helps relieve anxiety created by the pressure of task demands. Looking at a huge "To Do" list is overwhelming and anxiety provoking. When all assignments and steps to complete them are entered into a planner and balanced with chores, appointments and free time, it is clear that if the plan is followed, all of the work will get done on time. So once everything is planned and written in the planner, the only thing to be concerned about is what must be completed on any single day.

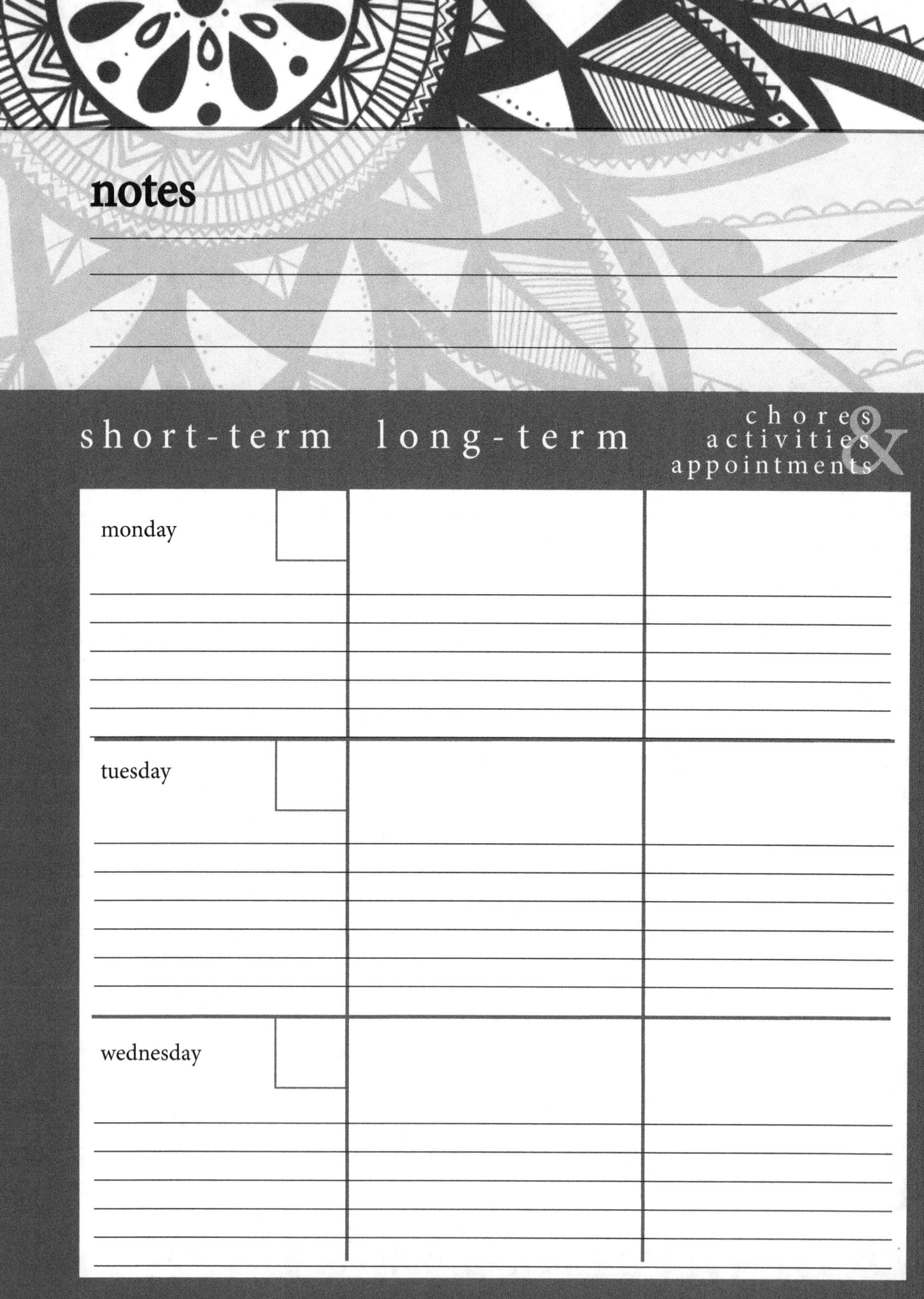

notes

short-term long-term

chores & activities appointments

monday		

tuesday		

wednesday		

thursday

friday

saturday

sunday

notes

_____
_____
_____
_____

short-term long-term

monday

tuesday

wednesday

thursday

friday

saturday

sunday

notes

_____

_____

_____

_____

short-term	long-term	chores & activities appointments
monday		
tuesday		
wednesday		

thursday

friday

saturday

sunday

notes

_____
_____
_____
_____

short-term	long-term	chores & activities appointments
monday		
tuesday		
wednesday		

thursday

friday

saturday

sunday

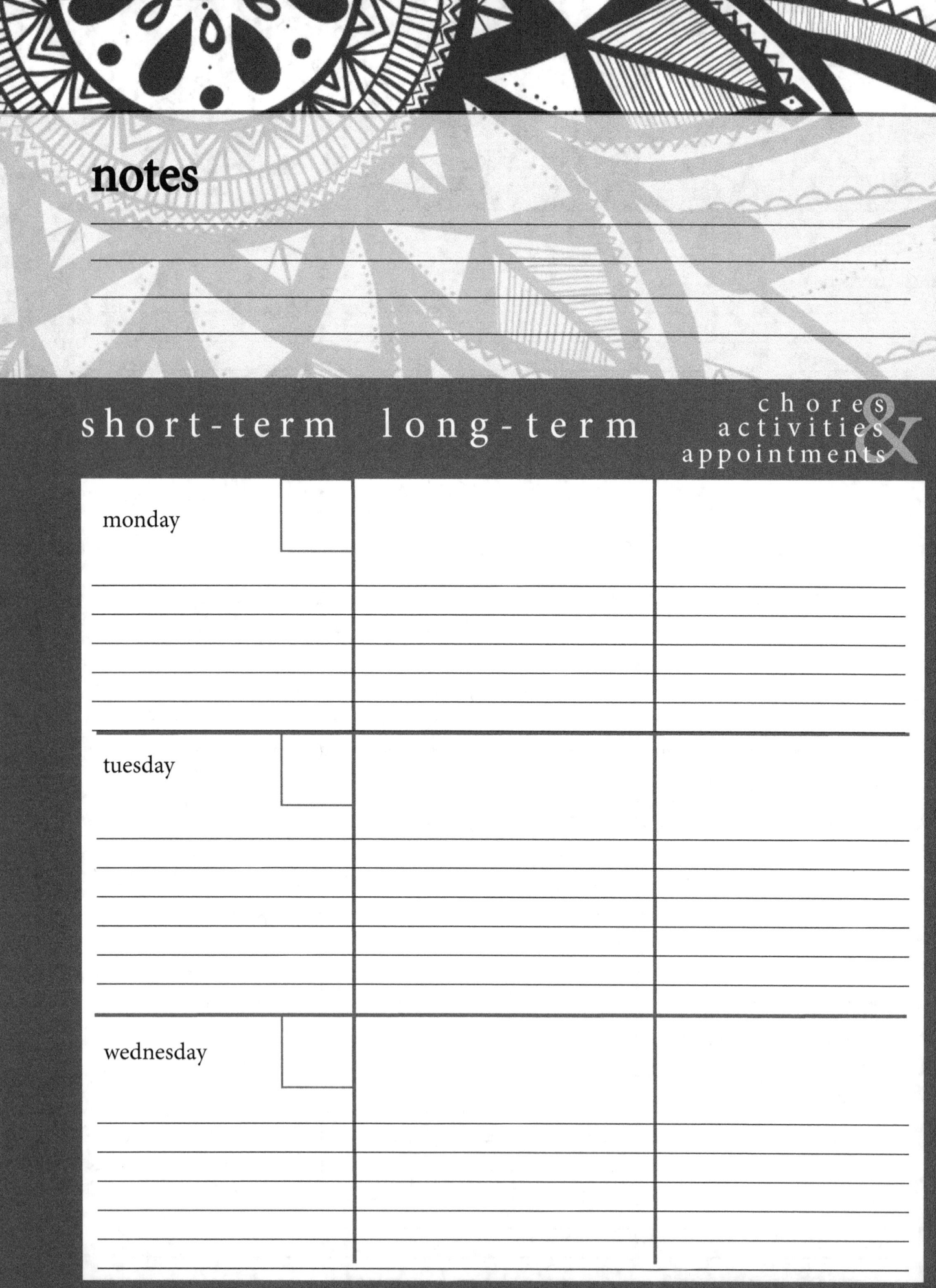

notes

short-term long-term

monday

tuesday

wednesday

thursday

friday

saturday

sunday

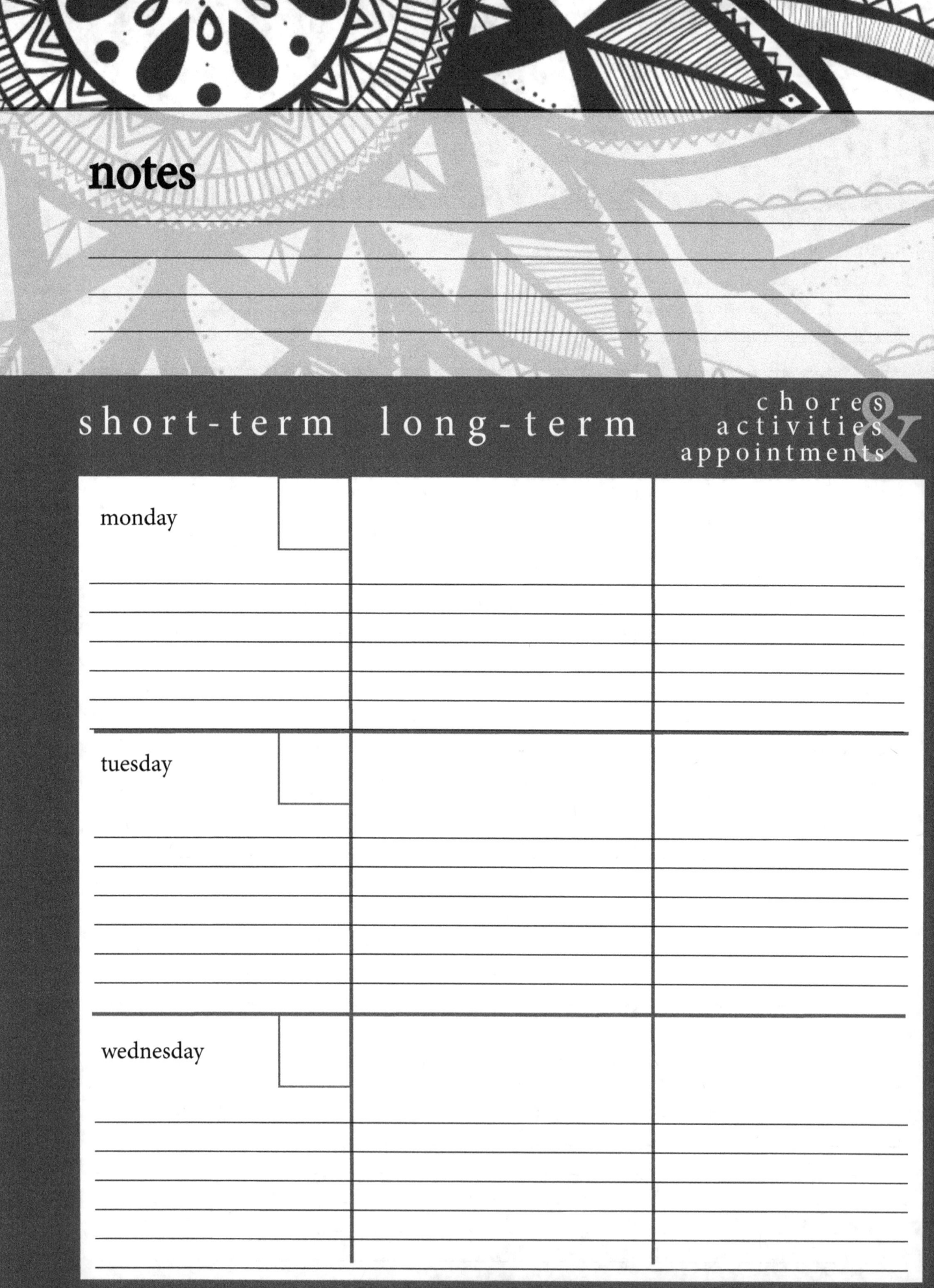

notes

_____

_____

_____

_____

short-term long-term		chores activities & appointments
monday		
tuesday		
wednesday		

thursday

friday

saturday

sunday

notes

_____

_____

_____

_____

short-term long-term   c h o r e s
                                         a c t i v i t i e s &
                                         appointments

monday		
tuesday		
wednesday		

thursday

friday

saturday

sunday

notes

_____

_____

_____

_____

short-term long-term		chores & activities appointments
monday		
tuesday		
wednesday		

thursday

friday

saturday

sunday

notes

_____

_____

_____

_____

short-term **long-term** chores
activities &
appointments

monday			
tuesday			
wednesday			

thursday

friday

saturday

sunday

notes

_____

_____

_____

_____

short-term long-term

monday		

tuesday		

wednesday		

thursday

friday

saturday

sunday

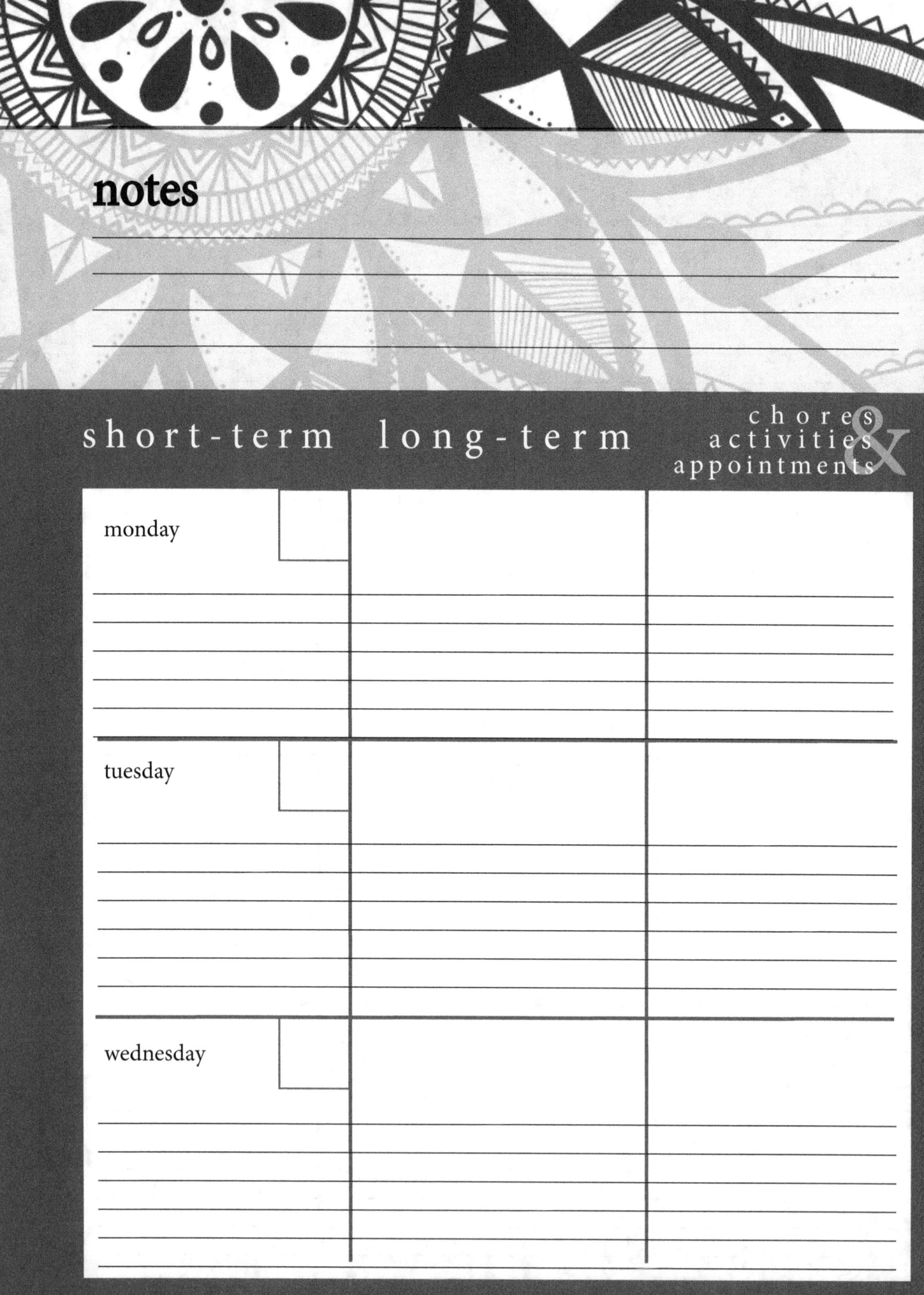

notes

_____

_____

_____

_____

short-term long-term

monday

tuesday

wednesday

thursday

friday

saturday

sunday

notes

_____
_____
_____
_____

short-term	long-term	chores & activities appointments
monday		
tuesday		
wednesday		

short-term   long-term

thursday

friday

saturday

sunday

notes

_____
_____
_____
_____

short-term long-term | chores & activities appointments

monday		
tuesday		
wednesday		

thursday

friday

saturday

sunday

notes

_____

_____

_____

_____

short-term   long-term   chores
                                    activities
                                    &appointments

monday		

tuesday		

wednesday		

thursday

friday

saturday

sunday

notes

_____
_____
_____
_____

short-term   long-term

monday		

tuesday		

wednesday		

thursday

friday

saturday

sunday

notes

_____

_____

_____

_____

monday		
_____		
_____		
_____		
_____		

tuesday		
_____		
_____		
_____		
_____		

wednesday		
_____		
_____		
_____		
_____		

thursday

friday

saturday

sunday

notes

_____
_____
_____
_____

short-term	long-term	chores & activities appointments
monday		
tuesday		
wednesday		

thursday

friday

saturday

sunday

notes

_____

_____

_____

_____

short-term   long-term

monday		
tuesday		
wednesday		

thursday

friday

saturday

sunday

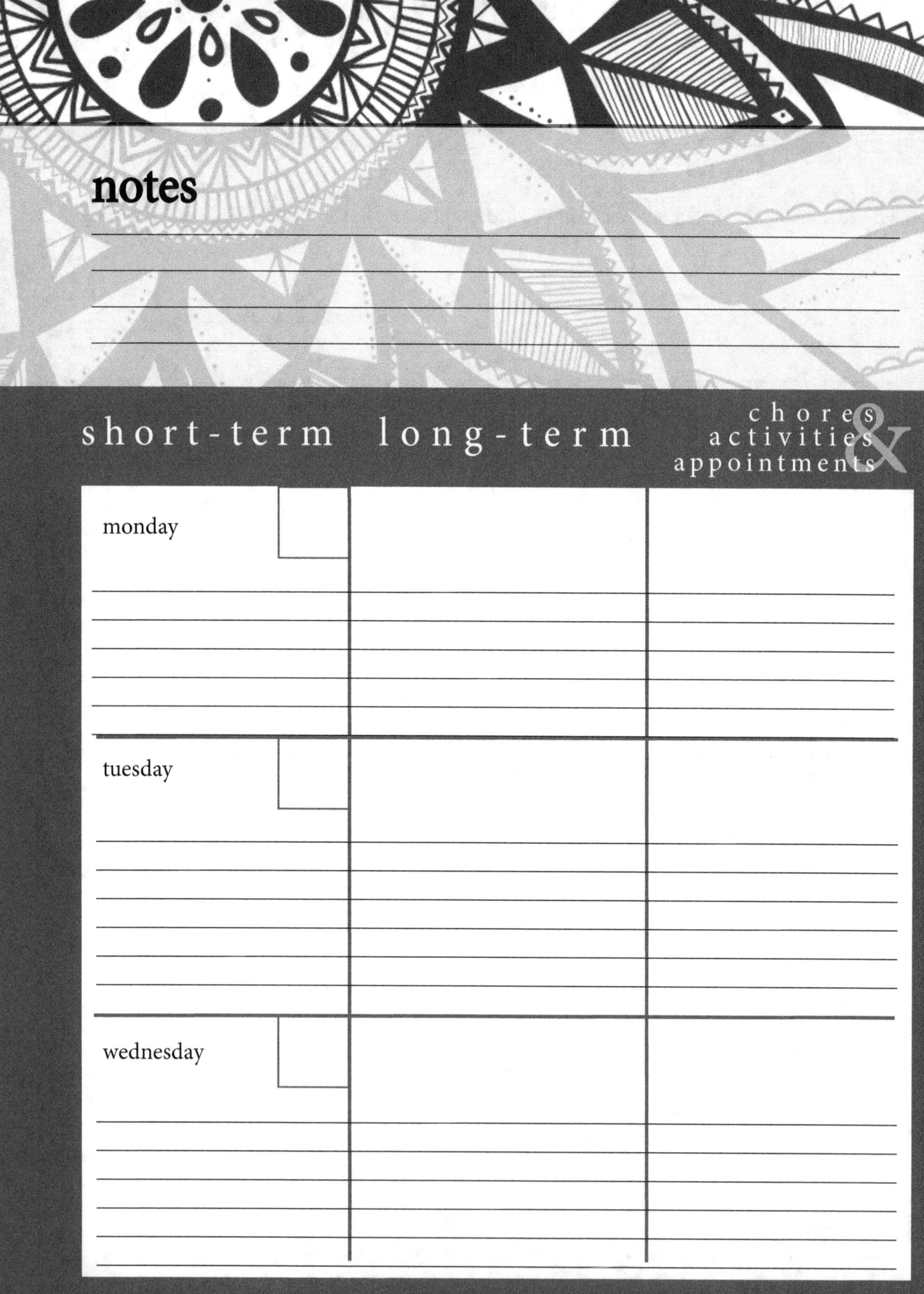

notes

short-term   long-term

chores
activities &
appointments

monday

tuesday

wednesday

thursday

friday

saturday

sunday

notes

_____

_____

_____

_____

short-term long-term

monday			

tuesday			

wednesday			

thursday

friday

saturday

sunday

notes

_____
_____
_____
_____

chores
activities **&**
appointments

monday		

tuesday		

wednesday		

thursday

friday

saturday

sunday

notes

_____
_____
_____
_____

short-term long-term

chores
activities
appointments
&

monday		
tuesday		
wednesday		

thursday

friday

saturday

sunday

notes

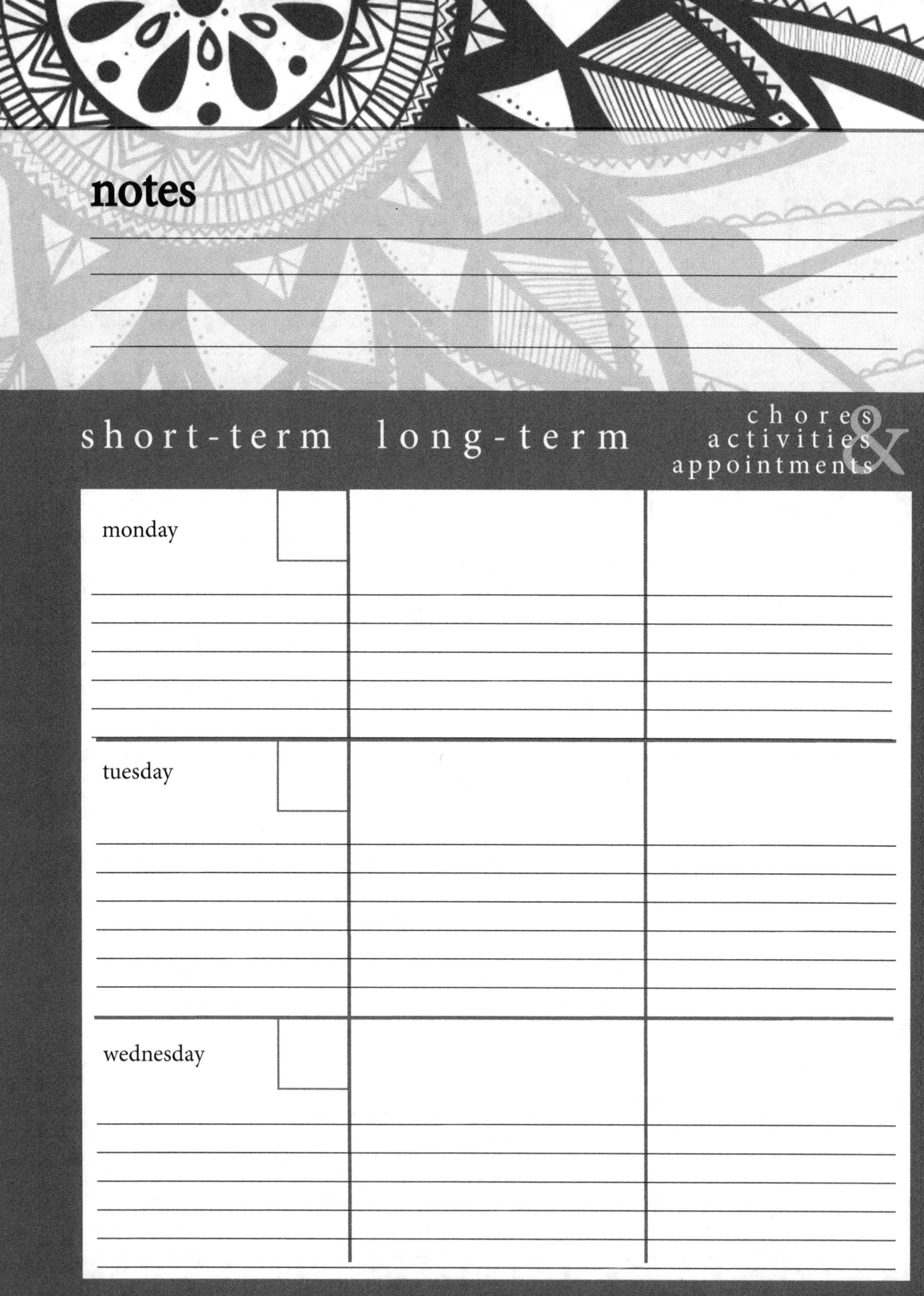

short-term	long-term	chores activities appointments &
monday		
tuesday		
wednesday		

thursday

friday

saturday

sunday

notes

_____

_____

_____

_____

short-term long-term

monday		

tuesday		

wednesday		

thursday

friday

saturday

sunday

notes

_____
_____
_____
_____

short-term long-term

c h o r e s
a c t i v i t i e s &
a p p o i n t m e n t s

monday
_____
_____
_____
_____

tuesday
_____
_____
_____
_____
_____

wednesday
_____
_____
_____
_____

thursday

friday

saturday

sunday

notes

_____

_____

_____

_____

short-term   long-term   chores activities appointments &

monday

_____
_____
_____
_____

tuesday

_____
_____
_____
_____
_____

wednesday

_____
_____
_____
_____

thursday

friday

saturday

sunday

notes

_____
_____
_____
_____

monday		

tuesday		

wednesday		

thursday

friday

saturday

sunday

notes

_____

_____

_____

_____

monday		

tuesday		

wednesday		

thursday

friday

saturday

sunday

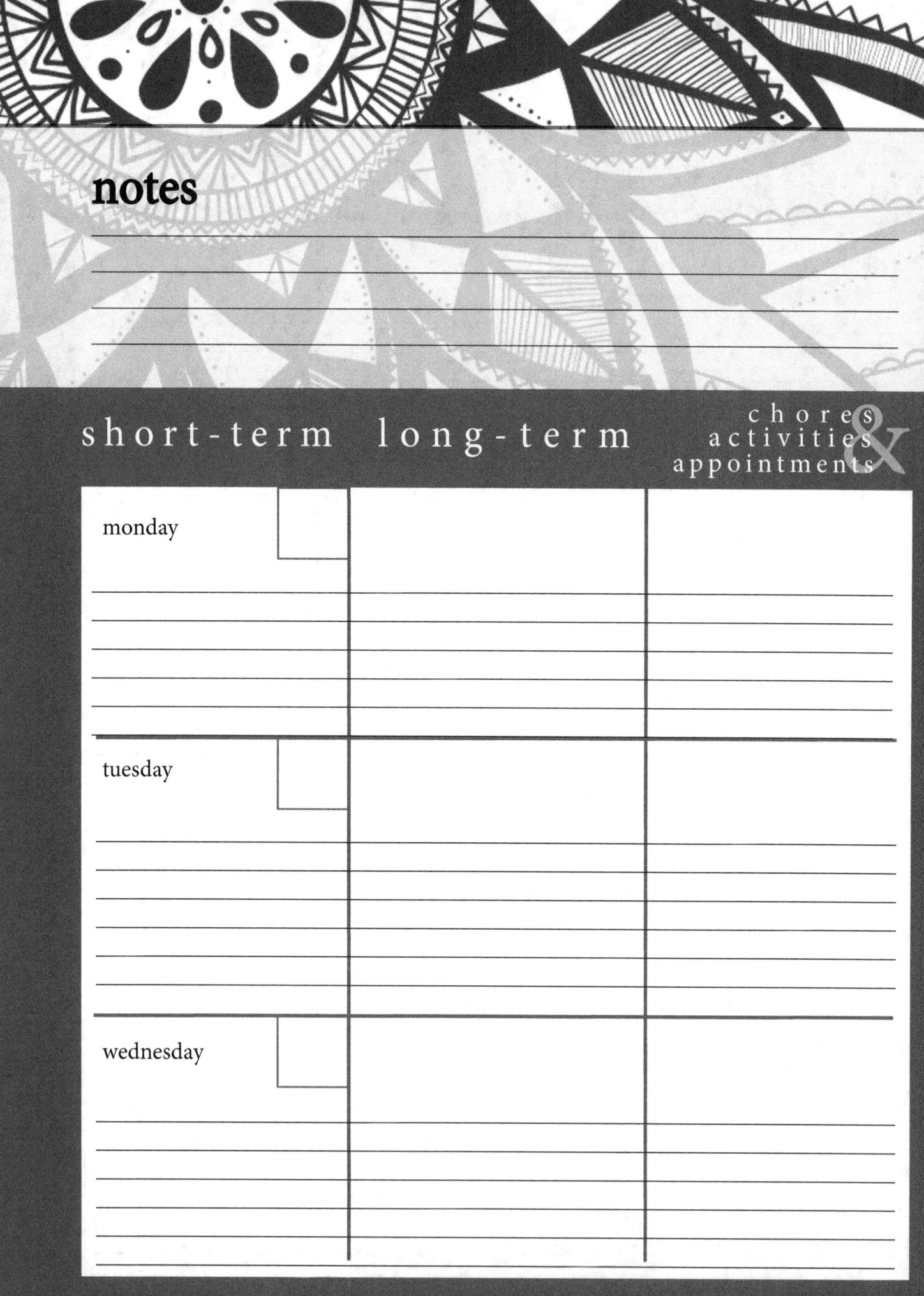

notes

short-term long-term

chores &
activities
appointments

monday			

tuesday			

wednesday			

thursday

friday

saturday

sunday

notes

_____
_____
_____
_____

chores & activities appointments

monday		

tuesday		

wednesday		

thursday

friday

saturday

sunday

notes

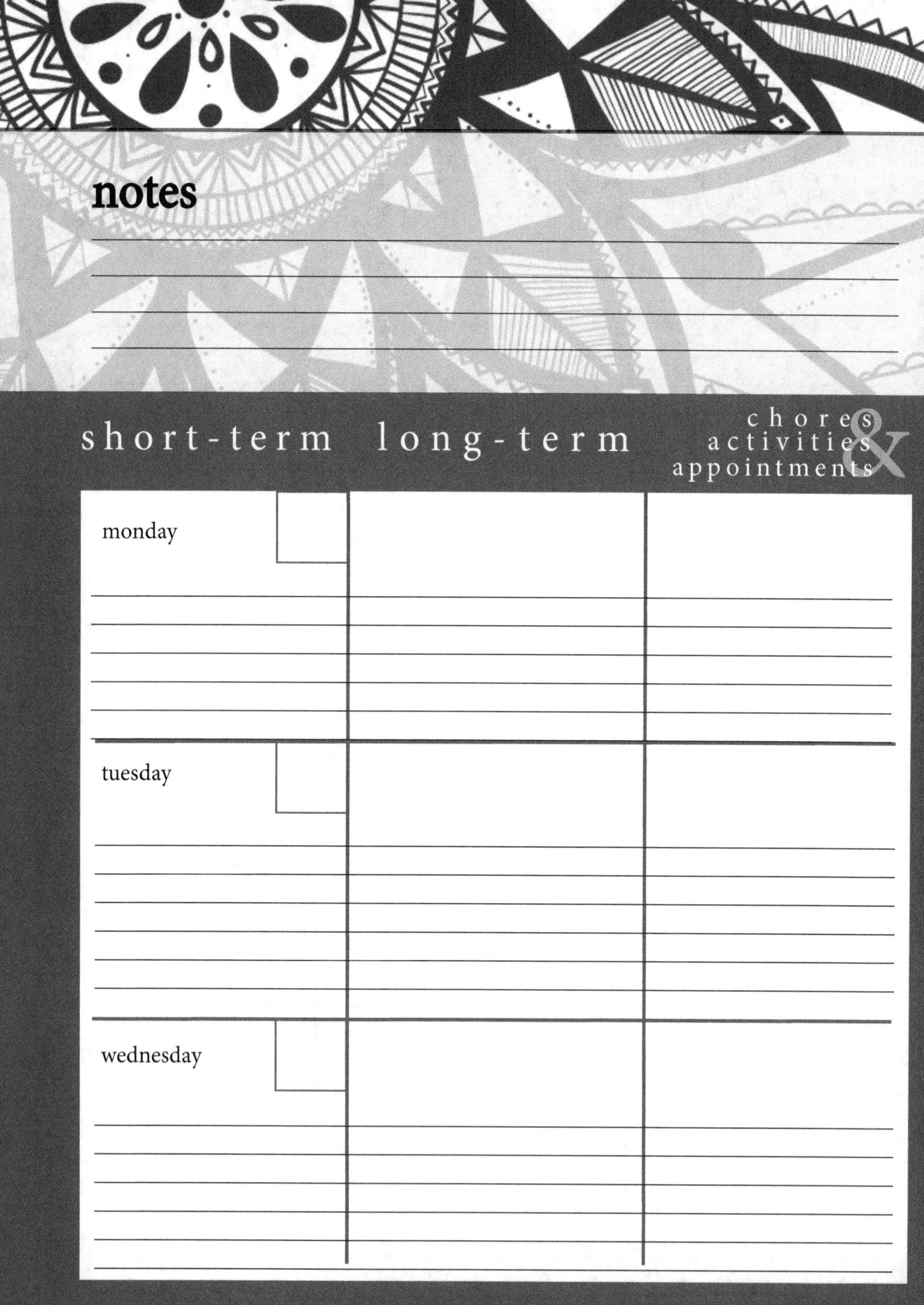

short-term long-term

chores
activities
appointments
&

monday

tuesday

wednesday

thursday

friday

saturday

sunday

notes

monday		

tuesday		

wednesday		

thursday

friday

saturday

sunday

notes

_____

_____

_____

_____

chores & activities appointments

monday		
tuesday		
wednesday		

chores
activities
appointments
&

thursday

friday

saturday

sunday

notes

_____

_____

_____

_____

monday

_____

_____

_____

_____

tuesday

_____

_____

_____

_____

wednesday

_____

_____

_____

_____

thursday

friday

saturday

sunday

notes

_____
_____
_____
_____

short-term long-term

c h o r e s
a c t i v i t i e s &
a p p o i n t m e n t s

monday		
tuesday		
wednesday		

thursday

friday

saturday

sunday

notes

short-term long-term

chores & activities appointments

monday		

tuesday		

wednesday		

thursday

friday

saturday

sunday

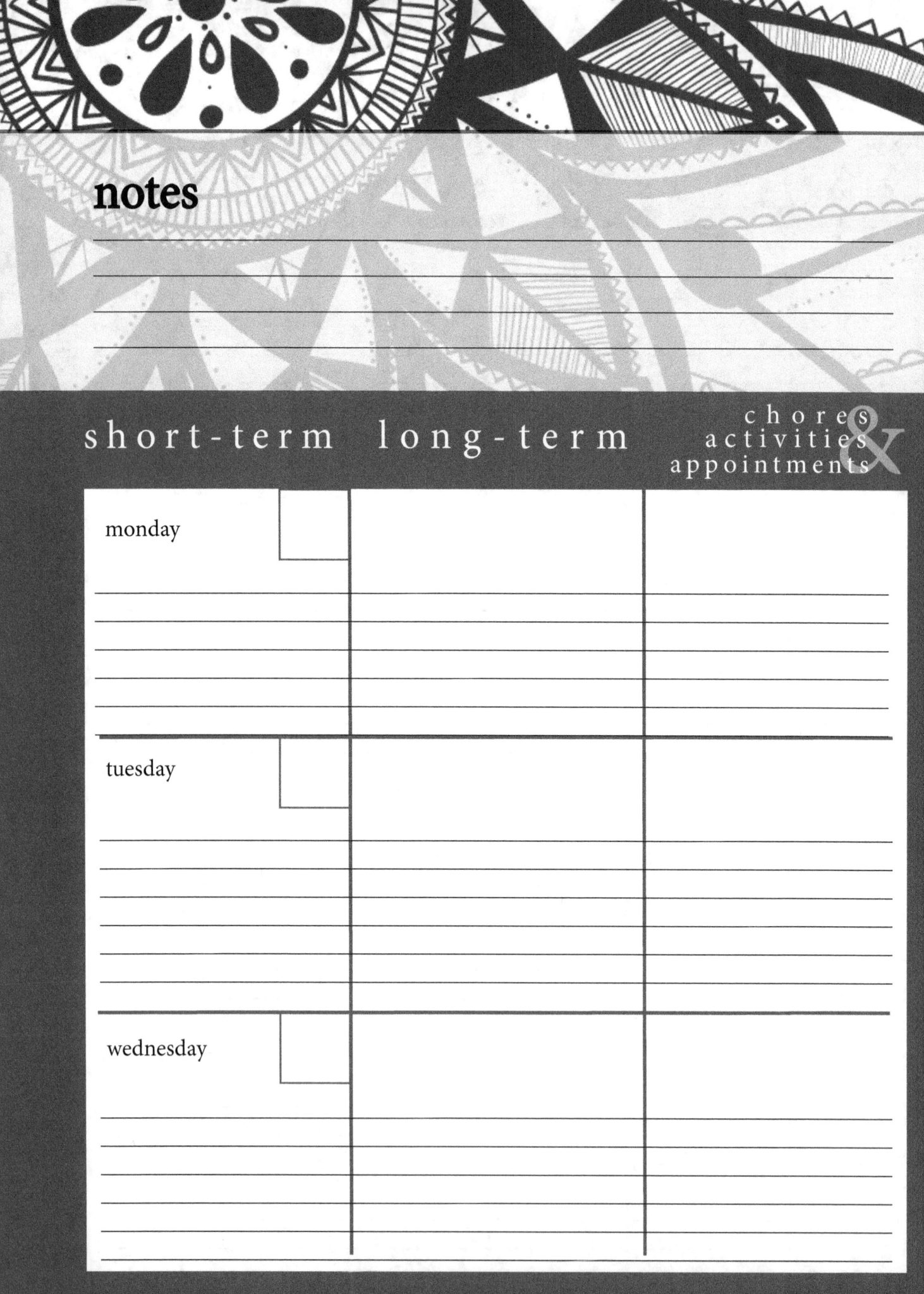

notes

_____

_____

_____

_____

short-term   long-term

chores
activities &
appointments

monday		
tuesday		
wednesday		

thursday

friday

saturday

sunday

notes

_____

_____

_____

_____

short-term long-term

monday

_____
_____
_____
_____

tuesday

_____
_____
_____
_____
_____

wednesday

_____
_____
_____
_____

thursday

friday

saturday

sunday

notes

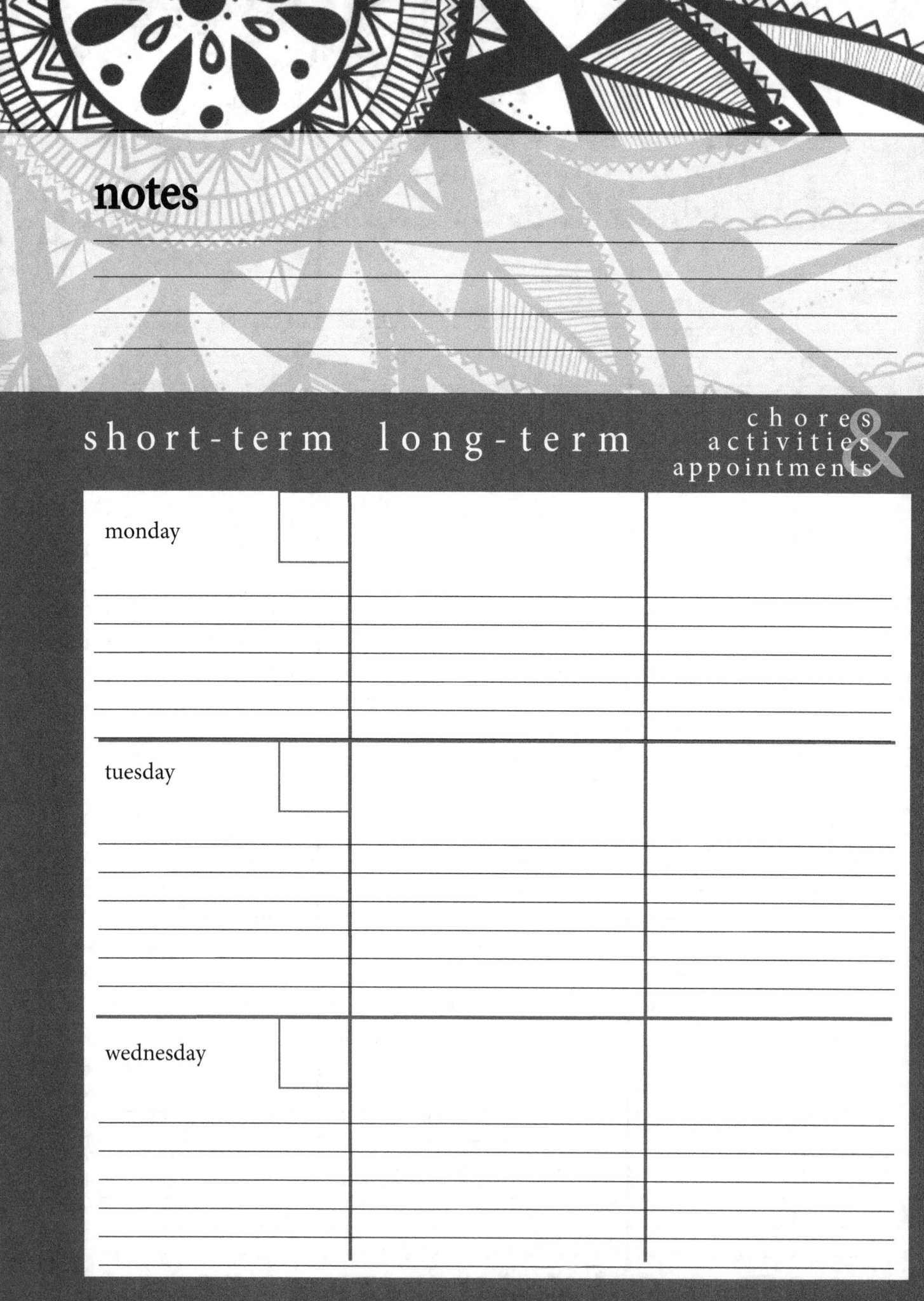

short-term long-term

monday		

tuesday		

wednesday		

thursday

friday

saturday

sunday

notes

_____
_____
_____
_____

chores
activities &
appointments

monday
_____
_____
_____
_____

tuesday
_____
_____
_____
_____

wednesday
_____
_____
_____
_____

thursday

friday

saturday

sunday

notes

_____

_____

_____

_____

monday		
tuesday		
wednesday		

thursday

friday

saturday

sunday

notes

_____

_____

_____

_____

chores
activities
appointments
&

monday		

tuesday		

wednesday		

thursday

friday

saturday

sunday

notes

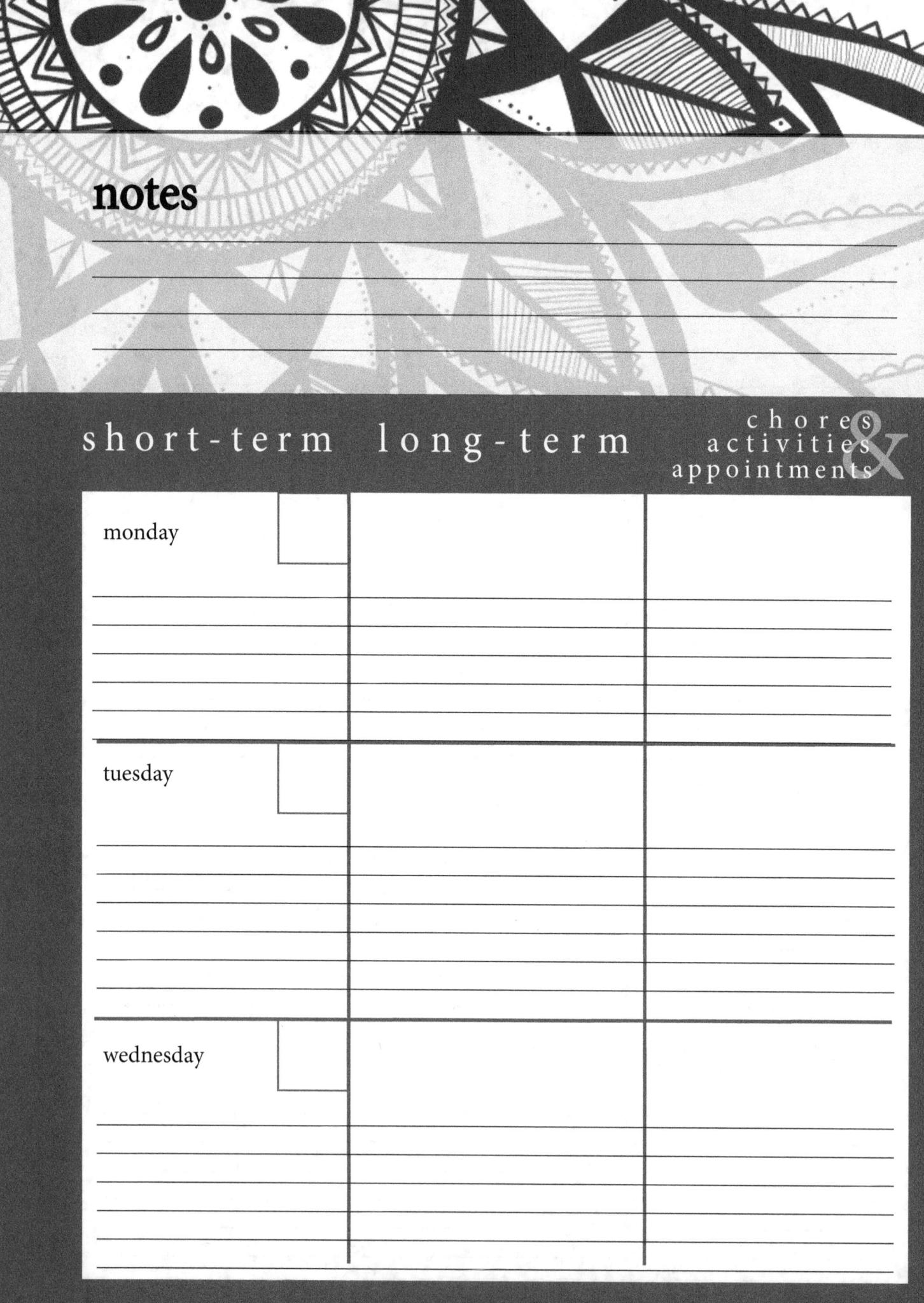

short-term long-term

chores
activities
appointments
&

monday

tuesday

wednesday

thursday

friday

saturday

sunday

notes

_____
_____
_____
_____
_____

monday		
tuesday		
wednesday		

short-term   **long-term**

activities &
appointments

thursday

friday

saturday

sunday

notes

_____

_____

_____

_____

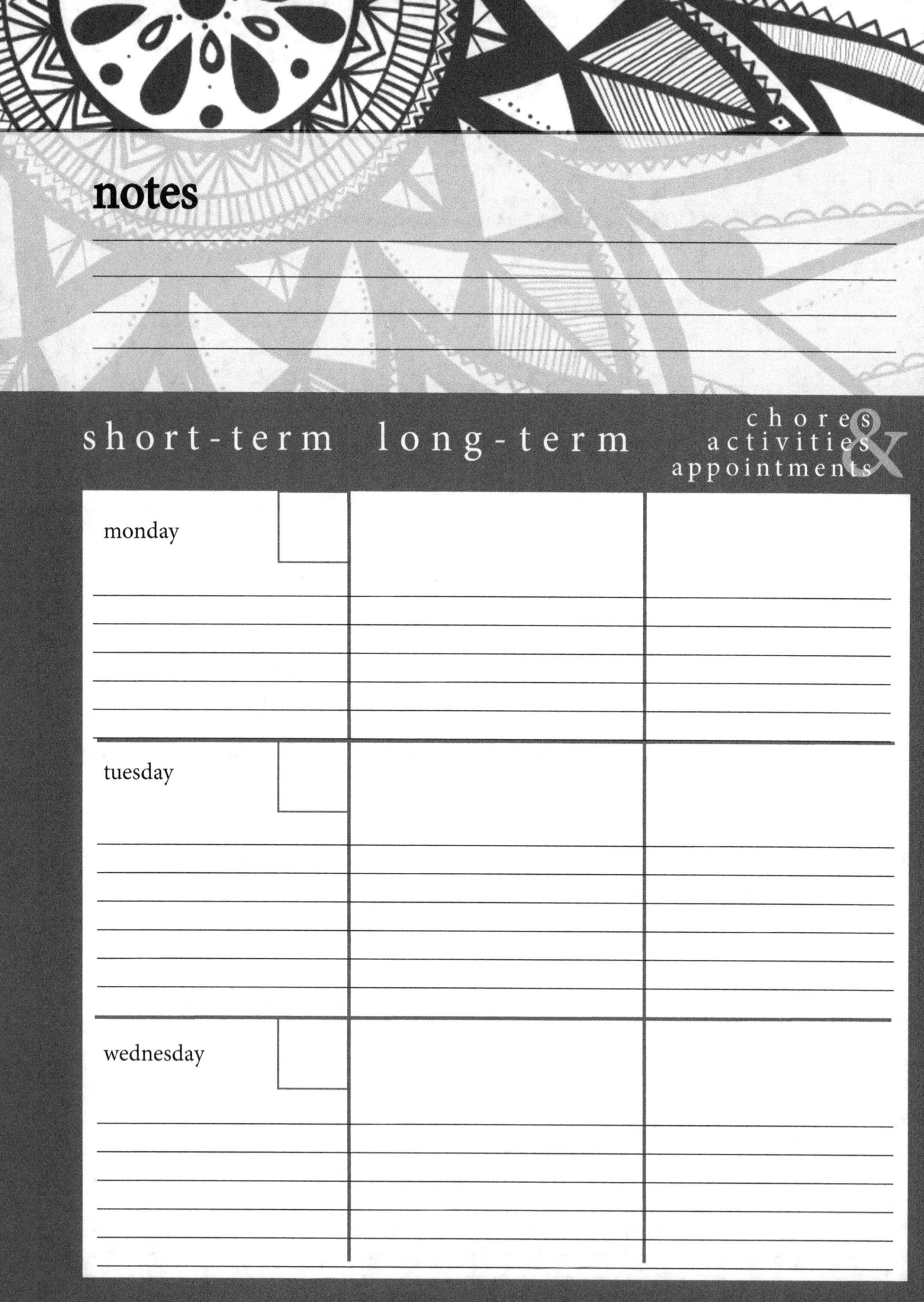

short-term	long-term	chores & activities appointments
monday		
tuesday		
wednesday		

thursday

friday

saturday

sunday

notes

_____
_____
_____
_____

monday		
tuesday		
wednesday		

thursday

friday

saturday

sunday

notes

chores & activities appointments

monday

tuesday

wednesday

thursday

friday

saturday

sunday

notes

_____

_____

_____

_____

monday

tuesday

wednesday

thursday

friday

saturday

sunday

notes

_____

_____

_____

_____

chores
activities
appointments
&

monday		
tuesday		
wednesday		

thursday

friday

saturday

sunday

notes

monday

tuesday

wednesday

thursday

friday

saturday

sunday

notes

_____

_____

_____

_____

monday		

tuesday		

wednesday		

thursday

friday

saturday

sunday

notes

_____
_____
_____
_____

short-term long-term

monday		
tuesday		
wednesday		

thursday

friday

saturday

sunday